SNOW HANGS ON THE BRANCHES OF EVERGREENS

Poems by
Stuart P. Radowitz

BLUE LIGHT PRESS ◆ 1ST WORLD PUBLISHING

1ST WORLD
PUBLISHING

SAN FRANCISCO ◆ FAIRFIELD ◆ DELHI

SNOW HANGS ON THE BRANCHES OF EVERGREENS
Copyright ©2020 Stuart P. Radowitz

BLUE LIGHT PRESS
www.bluelightpress.com
bluelightpress@aol.com

1ST WORLD PUBLISHING
PO Box 2211
Fairfield, IA 52556
www.1stworldpublishing.com

BOOK & COVER PHOTO & DESIGN
Melanie Gendron
melaniegendron999@gmail.com

AUTHOR PHOTO
Dr. Sherry Radowitz

FIRST EDITION

Library of Congress Control Number: 2020945803

ISBN: 9781421836737

for Jesse

Acknowledgments

A special thank you to Gabriella Laskaris for assistance in the preparation of this manuscript.

To Diane Frank for believing in my writing and still being a fan after fifty years.

And as always, for my wife Sherry.

Some of these poems first appeared in: *Ascent Aspirations; Bards Anthologies* 2018 and 2019; *Black Mountain Press – 64 Best Poets of 2018; Blue Moon Literary and Art Review; Calliope; Cold Mountain Review; Dappled Things; Ginosko; Molloy Literary Journal; Nassau County Poet Laureate Society Review –* Vol. III, V, VI, and VII; *Otis Nebula; Poets to Come: A Poetry Anthology in Celebration of Walt Whitman's Bicentennial;* and, *The Avocet:* Summer 2017, Summer 2018, Winter 2019, and Summer 2020.

Table of Contents

Places

It is late.

One, two in the morning.
Smoke licks its way up
over the heads of people.

Snow
usually covers
a place like this.

Here
it is cold
and raining.

It is early.
One,
two in the morning.

The road dissolves
in fog.

Away

One moon,
light on the road
to the first change.

Owl in the field,
white haze
in the moon's eye.

I follow either
rust fox over the hill
or blue smoke.

The way is moon and fox
for the moon and fox.
The way is clear.

Crystal Lake, CT.

for Jesse

Daylight wakes me
up and out and into the
what? Where am I going again?
Why does it always happen this way?

Monday morning, crystal clear air, crystal
lake out behind my house. The path
down to the boathouse slips with
rocks and loose dirt.

Every day is always like this. Up
and out, without you
all I can see are clouds.
All I can hear is your laugh.

Your eyes, blue gray exploding with life,
your shirt unbuttoned,
hair greased back,
that laugh, those eyes.

I hear you say, *I'll be back*
in a few minutes.
Heavy steps down the stairs,
the door slams.

Daylight drifts away, brings you back.
I can still remember that white car,
your olive skin,
waking without you.

Rockaway Beach

In the distance
ocean and bird
cut through the dune.
Across the dune
bony fingers
point off into the distance.

Three ships on the horizon,
distant barge and tanker
soundlessly sailing.
Who are they, the
sailors, seamen,
the captain?

Wooden piers
splintered and welcoming
stretch out their arms.
Gin, scotch and beer
on the long polished bar.
Slide down the glasses.

Drink up your fill.
Cheap boarded bungalows
to go home to.
The hardness of winter
air, clear gale winds
cross the face of streets.

Cold gale wind freezes time.
Explosions of violence
punch the street
hands cuffed, flashing lights
do rags that won't
come off.

Overhead low flying
planes in a parallel
arrangement with time.

Looking out over the bay,
first light, gulls
out for breakfast.
The strength of the ocean
swallows us every day.

Lives end here,
disappear into waves
that disappear.
Drowning people come here
to be saved and
are swept away, out to sea.

You, All of You, Me

In Taormina in Sicily
the ancient Roman amphitheater looks out
over the sea. Today
I saw your beauty for the first time.
I don't know what will happen next.
So many people are doing other things.
Finite possibilities, finite choices. Every way
leads to one ending.

It was nice to talk to you,
hear your voice, picture your face.
Certain things in life come with baggage
relationships, friendships, relatives.
Certain things come untangled but
not that many. Traffic, crowds, gas prices
are all entangled.

Driving through Venice Beach
we drove a little too far
and missed our exit.
Jugglers on the street tossed knives,
coming down sharp, pointed
ready to pierce your palm unless

you grab the handle.
The breeze on my back is soft and warm.
One of the last days of summer
driving past stone walls
I see you as you are.

How many times must death appear
before he comes for you, I mean me,
comes for me.

Finally, Cactus

Hummingbirds
have moved into my backyard.
Down at the shore, sand

piles to the boardwalk.
Surfers and gulls and volleyball on the dunes.
Yesterday's compromise seems like a dream.

Overhead
green canopy growth
acts as a mirror or a window into your heart.

Loose cactus leaves flat on the ground, rooting.

Falling River Falling Rain

Water washes away this pain
over the earth.

Roots, pebbles, stones, leaves
clear light filters through tall windows.

Bent and angled wind
dusts the light, pelts rain,
turns the river.

Out of the ash of brown cactus
a green spore, a finger.
New growth begins.

Rushing Winds, Crushing Waves

Everything is time.
A year in the Himalayas. Six months in Brooklyn
walking up and down steps
to the next floor.

It's like playing a shell game.
What's behind the next door?
A lake house with small dock
sloping lawn down to the water.

A mountain home, fat logs and log furniture,
a small stream crossed with rocks.
The canopy still green
in late October.

A fisherman in Cold Spring Harbor
living upstairs in a salt box,
downstairs a tavern. Outside
rushing winds, crushing waves.

The Lake Behind My House

Time distorts the years.
All the names of people whose names
I can't remember come to mind.

Was it five or fifteen?
You don't have to look at yourself in a mirror
to know what's inside.

A poet friend,
wrote a book about trekking the Himalayas.
She quoted a Buddhist hiker who says,

the miracle is the moment.
Every hour is a luxury.
All the world's wealth is in the sky.

Framed by clear sunlight
earth air water fire woods
surround the lake behind my house.

The Weather Can Take Your Life

The weather can take your life.
Cancer can take your life.
Pancreatic cancer spreads quickly
through your body like silver veins
reaching out.

The weather can take your life.
Ice, snow, slippery roads
can take your life.
The moon can take your life.

A full moon glowing on a clear night
and a crescent moon between clouds
can take your life.
Danger can take your life.

Boredom can take your life.
Being alone can take your life.
Or alone in a crowd, spinning
out of control until the only thing left

is not having that life.
The weather can take your life.
Heat in Florida, the tropics,
the mountains of Santa Fe, Taos Pueblo

can take your life. The chill
of North Dakota and Custer's Last Battlefield
and wildfires can take your life.

A bad doctor, a hospital emergency room
a hospital infection, bleach
can take your life. Drowning,

gasping, reaching out, looking inward
can take your life.
The weather can take your life.
Thorns pricking your finger will kill you.

The heart stopping, lungs closing
will take your life.
Running into an abandoned building
and not getting out of an abandoned building
will take your life.
Strapped to a gurney will kill you.

Therapy sessions and therapy sessions
and not going to therapy sessions
will take your life.
The weather will kill you.
The weather will take your life.

Hit by a car crossing Queens Blvd.,
smashing your car into a tree,
trees smashing into you, colliding
with your right of way

will take your life.
The fire dept. will take your life.
Flames and fire and heat,
crumbling buildings and alley ways

after a Broadway show will take your life.
A yellow school bus or silver plane
diving out of the sky will take your life.
Warm spring afternoons will take your life.

Seasons changing back and forth,
faster and slower will take your life.
Sleeping alone, or waking alone, running
from dreams and falling down stairs

will take your life.
Dreaming of sleep, and dreaming of death,
being somewhere or not being really there
will take your life.

Early morning will take your life.
Harsh words like "get out of here"
or "leave me alone" or "stop"
will take your life.

The weather will take your life.
Rough seas and fisherman's rough hands
will take your life.

Going to sleep or waking up and
not sleeping will take your life.
The weather will kill you.

Trail Ridge Road

Fossilized leaves in the shale. Trees
half green with things that never happen.
Everything about your body
pillows my head and opens my soul.

Driving over Trail Ridge Road
in Rocky Mountain National Park
we pass through time.
It could be 1854.

The road narrows to one lane.
A car comes in the opposite direction.
We pull over on the shoulder
inches from a thousand-foot drop.

When the cactus blew away
I didn't know it was bad luck.
Sometimes the signs around us
are hard to see.

Vision

My hand brushes against your cheek.
Your hand barely flicks away
a long thin strand of brown hair.
Leaves rustle as I touch you.

Branches snap as we talk in soft whispers.
A sunburst of light opens, finally
I can see you again.
Smooth white legs wrapped around
a bicycle, draped over handlebars,
tangled in vines and picnic baskets.

My hand nearly brushes against your cheek.
Your lips tell me why my eyes
look into your soul.

I see your heart and almost touch it.
Your fingers spread across my back.
I roll over in the grass.
All our time together floats
on the back of a dragonfly.

Babylon

In the heat of summer
petals peel back and flowers open.
Spiky needles and delicate barbs keep
all away but a white butterfly
balanced in the air, briefly
stopping, dancing, longing
for more.

The flower of Babylon is turquoise and silver,
lime green and starfish.
Waves of sunlight wash over
thousands of tiny shells and seabirds.
Cormorants and horseshoe crab
stand at the edge of the bay.

Sandy bottoms need to be brushed.
Gentle hands wipe away tears.
The seabird's song to her young says
Fly over land, away from the waves,
to the flowers we saw nearby.
The starfish rests in the shallows.

The flower of Babylon peeks
out at the dawn, rolls over
and dreams of starfish and sunlight.
A wisp of light brown hair nests
over a bent arm, shoulder,
neck.

Beads of sweat moisten the morning.
Flecks of silver and green and gold jump
over the waves, the rocks, the blanket.

Window sills look out
to the garden and the shore beyond.
Stars dance in the early morning light
so that we can sleep.

The flower of Babylon unfolds against the breeze.
We too think we can be as fresh, as beautiful,
as open.
Dreams of white clouds and a sleeping starfish,
a peaceful child.
The sand ripples beneath us.
The purple sunrise says wake up.

Dania Beach

for Andrew

Ripples of sky and blue water
surround us.
Loss at sea is irreversible.
Clouds that once were here
never come back.

The heat beats down and down and down.
The saltiness of green ocean water fills lungs
and spills out over onto the deck.
Sails furl and unfurl, flap and wave

as if that could bring you back.
Rescue parties come and go
board and search, wave, signal, flag,
radio. Static crackles, points to the horizon,
disappears behind tanker wash.

Tomorrow we search again, fresh
from dreams of mountain lakes,
canyon streams, inland valleys.
We say the ocean has done this,
never ending, a blinding light
lost forever.

Key West

Out there, surrounded by
ripples of sky and blue water
ripples of blue sky and deep water

searching for your heart
clinging to your soul
drifting through days,
drifting by fishermen's nets, tangled.

I carry your heart
loving your nearness
clinging to you.

The roundness of your cheeks
the freshness of your seas
splintered galleons half submerged.

Your heart swings away
your soul caught in nets

the closeness of flesh
the mist of your breath.

Total disregard for everything,
everyone. Every sea carries you,
distant horizon fading.

Your Window

Your window
black without you
one eye open, one eye shut

daisies,
black eyed peas, sunflowers
bursting with seed.

Your leap of faith
across continents, floating
down alpine meadows

covered in snow, spring
shoots poking up,
fingers beckoning

lifelines, arms stretched
to catch you, to
cradle you

to rock you forever.

In the Minutes Before Sleep

In the minutes before sleep
my chest pressed against your back
my knees tucked into the crease of your knees

a gentle darkness,
burnt orange leaves float downward,
a blanket of soft golden red.

I touch the side of your face.
Your arms fold over your breasts.
I smell your hair and the pores of your skin,
vanilla almond.

The soft morning light reveals
a river of blue between drifting clouds,
your face, a blue jay, a white pine fence.

The Girl on the Train

I see your face
in the girl on the train
to Manhattan, the girl with long hair
in Vincent's Clam Bar.

Fine, go ahead, evaluate me.
We've already discussed you,
your skin, your neck, your
long brown hair, your
legs, your hips, the bend
in the back of your knees.

What we haven't talked about
are the aches that you feel,
the sharp sticking pain
in your heart as if
someone poked a thumb
into all your chambers

tearing skin, rough and burning
an irritation like the sand
inside an oyster that becomes
a pearl, two pearls.
The heartache of love and children and family

motherhood struggles,
as if walking against the wind
or digging out of a snowbank,
as if a pin pricked your heart while
you try to shovel your way out of a storm.

The burning redness, rough
as concrete, hard as stones
the river has not yet washed smooth.

A stone worker's hands maybe
or a dishwasher's, burnt and red
scalding water, steel wool,
pots too heavy to lift.

The chef calls out, *table three,*
bring this to table three.
Too late for a quiet night.
Too late for the smoothness
of stones, of breasts, of cheeks.

A Single Sliced Strawberry

I made you lunch today.
A small salad with spinach, romaine,
creamy white mozzarella,
a sliced hardboiled egg.

If we could sit and talk
I would tell you about my house,
the stonework from Pennsylvania and Vermont
my den with its soft leather couch,
the rough travertine from Italy,
the white maple desk where I sit
and write this to you.

A small cup, maybe half an ounce of honey mustard dressing.
The couch is a cocoa colored brown,
brandy or cognac or chestnut colored.
The travertine is light, natural, different shades,
earthy with a slightly darker grout.
Half a sliced plum tomato.

If we could sit and talk
I would tell you about the time
I wished you were here
before I even knew you.

When you walk down the stairs to my family room
you would see all the pictures of my son,
dark hair, olive skin, at fifteen playing hockey,
twenty-one with his sister, twenty-five handsome and strong,
smiling.

I made you dinner tonight.
Thin lightly breaded eggplant, warm
tomato slices, a small bowl of pasta.

If we could sit and talk
I would tell you about
the creative writing class I teach at night.
Thoughtful students, pens, a retired female undercover detective
in green leather pants suit, black beret.

She would play the hooker, like on TV
and her back up would bust the john.
An off-Broadway playwright, struggling
thirty years of monologues on his shelves,
so many one-night performances.
A performance artist, loud, crashing, dramatic.
A thin blonde wisp of a girl who loves life,
loves people, gives of her love to others.
A single mom, young, struggling, proud.

If we could sit and talk
I would tell you about
all the cars I have ever owned, Volkswagen
Jeep, Scout, Porsche, Blazer. I would tell you about
high school in Brooklyn, walking down Kings Highway
on a Friday night, Jahn's ice cream parlor
near Erasmus, the first school in Brooklyn,
and the Flatbush Ave. church with its tall spire.
What Bay Ridge was like, and Canarsie.
College in Syracuse, graduate school in Colorado
where places became so important.

A green vegetable, broccoli steamed, still crisp.
If we could sit and talk
I would tell you about today, everything
white with snow, icy
wind driving snow down my neck.
You making snow angels, snowmen.

The littlest children beat you in snowball fights.
The littlest children flash so brightly and pelt you with love.
Laughing, freezing, wet, soaked to the skin
socks come off and dry towels warm small feet.

For dessert the smallest piece of chocolate cake,
soft vanilla ice cream, a single sliced strawberry.

Glimpse of Your Heart

What is it about your face
that grabbed me, twisted my arm,
said don't let go?

I give you small gifts
a wind chime, golden aspen
incense from the bodega
crackers, salty and dry for your hunger.

Sleeping with you,
my chest to your back,
my leg to the back of your legs
my face up against your neck

smelling your hair,
feeling it against my face
arm under your shoulder,
over your chest, wrapped
around all of you.

Holding you, hearing your breath
waking with you, disheveled hair
soft wrinkly pajamas.

I say your name over and over.
An early winter storm rages outside.
Wind clashes with wind, gusts
push gusts. Like the storm
we too shall come to an end.

Afternoon in Mykonos

When we went up into the hills of Mykonos,
barefoot, by bus, baked by the sun
last ones on, hanging out the door
overlooking the harbor, the fishing boats
pastel blue and green and yellow skiffs
dot the shoreline.

From the narrow twisted road
splintered decks, fingers hooked and raw
lives filled with cold damp mornings,
wet meals, fish for breakfast
fish for lunch.

Pear shaped Greek women cutting tomatoes
slicing onion and cucumber, crumbling feta
as if Vesuvius herself had spoken and said
feed the men, feed the children
kiss the hearts of daughters.

Taos Pueblo

Anasazi men turn inward
in the desert heat
of August.

Summer won't last, winter
turns to cold ice
slushy snow.

Running through the desert
my footprints disappear.
This place without me is still.

Metal garbage cans, stone patio blocks,
the softness of cedar, growing.
Sometimes you hear the wind and nothing more.

I hear your voice.
Why are you here? You asked me.
I ask myself the same question.

I feel the sun beating on my back.

Amsterdam

In Amsterdam
canals circle the city.
Marjorie, the girl in the house on the canal
walks back and forth in front of her windows,
from room to room,
she stops and sits down on her couch.

Thinking about the loneliness that circles the city,
the haze she sometimes
finds herself in,
thinking about how pure sunlight
streams through her windows,
thinking about waking in the morning,
alone.

In Amsterdam
seagulls at six o'clock
bark out at the fresh breeze,
the clouds, the brown rippled water.
Church bells announce
small cobblestones, ancient brick,
splashes of sunlight.

She goes out into the sunlight,
into the light of change.
The weather, so much a part
of who we are.
The dark clouds and bright sunlight
color us.
The morning breeze
blows hope into our eyes.

Norway

Lonely
in a small town.
Fog so thick the fjord disappears.
Change comes early and often.
In the distance freighters and their foghorns.
Rain lashes our cabin.
Adrift in a volcanic lake,
Geiranger Fjord reaches up.

Lana thinks life must be better
somewhere else.
She says she is moving to a big city
to hear the noise, see the people,
smell the streets and the buses.
She says, *the Seven Sisters hold me here,*
but her brother says *no, you must go.*

She says, *people need people.*
It is no good to always be alone.
I want to be lost in a crowd.
Spin out of control in the middle of hundreds.
Her brother says, *Norway is not for you,*
there is too much ice, too many cold days.

Lana says, *I will call you from New York,*
call you from London, call you at night.
You must tell me everything that has happened,
every flake of snow that has fallen,
every sound that you have heard.
How cold it is. How cold it will be.

This way my heart will be free
and my eyes able to stare into the sun.

Lake Olden

Your face vanishes.

I leave the physical world
and search for you.
Your outline appears to me and then your body.

You look good, full, alive, happy.
A smile on your face.
A million miles away, but still here.

There is no tomorrow.

We become like the glaciers.
Encased in ice, frozen
even on the hottest days.

Eventually we melt and form a pool
a lake, a calm surface of water.
Everything goes on forever.

Gentle Light

Flights of geese
circle the field, sometimes flying off
before they will land.

When I saw you in the shower
for the first time
water beading on your back,
your shoulders,
white porcelain tile surrounding you.
The warmth of steam and spray.

Three acres may not be much land
but it's peaceful. Your spirit
bathes me in gentle light. The warmth
of steam and spray, shadows falling
across your face.

The geese land six or eight at a time
until there are hundreds on the ground.
They stay until the dogs come.
7 a.m. walking your dog.
Smoking a cigarette.
Cigarette smoke in the shadows.

The geese take flight
like burning stars
shooting across the sky
and then gone.

End of Spring

The end of spring happens
quietly unannounced
in the early morning.

When no one is thinking
it wakes you with a gasp.

All is still.
The small house on Overland Trail has no heat.
The big house on Long Island takes you back.
Wind blows the white pine hard.

The White Farmhouse

The farmhouse was white, surrounded
thirteen acres, mostly open, some wooded.
A small pond, an acre and a half
in the back, a well
one hundred fifty feet deep.

Drinking water flowed up
from an ancient underground stream.
Deer knew it was a safe place to graze.
A red fox often loped by,
as if going somewhere.

When you said hello this morning,
I kissed your shoulder.
Our house is warm, though in the winter
it was not always so.

Thursday a gray dove landed under the white pine.
She was looking for a safe place to die.
Friday morning she had moved nearer to the pond
to a place where two sections of fence meet.

When you said good night I went out,
put my finger in the well and touched
the rough damp brick.

The red fox came by again
but did not touch the dove.
No one was hungry enough to eat.

2 a.m. Austin, Texas

2 a.m. Austin, Texas
a room full of strangers,
smoky and loud.

I slip out into the night
full white moon
chilled morning air,
vapor in the dawn mist.

Downtown blocks the view of open fields.
Open fields surround my heart
space for you to come in.
Space for me to look out.

Thirty miles north of Austin
a small house on a wooded hillside
oatmeal bubbles on the stove
two young girls running behind a fence.

Two gray cats face each other
on a gray weather-beaten porch.
Everyone finds their own space
in the house, on the porch, in the yard.

Everyone speaks softly or giggles in low voices
walking up behind the house, through the woods
lifting up logs, looking under stones
for snakes, turtles, lizards.

Tree branches down
on the hillside, deer grazing.
I have done everything I can
to prepare for this.

Seed, plant, buckets of water.
At night their mother reads softly to them.
Lemony Snicket, Baby-Sitters Club
until they fall asleep.

Their brother comes to visit often,
making sure the girls and the women
are alright.
Everyone is relieved.

When he leaves he stops at
the Spanish bar, goes into the smoky room
to see his friends.
He stays until it is time for him to go.

3 a.m. Austin, Texas
open fields surround my heart
space for you to come in
space for me to look out.

Something is Changing

I look at my fingers,
at the veins
on the back of my hands,
at the darkening color
of my skin, at the veins
up and down my forearms.

I planted tomatoes.
Black ink irrigates the beds.
Inside and outside have become one.
The Oriole nest in my white pine
rains blue eggs.
Some survive. Some do not.

I have finally memorized the pieces
of my life and now
must forget it.
I have finally brought everything outside in
and turned everything inside
out for you to see.

Something is changing.
The Orioles, the Bluebirds, the cramps
in my legs at night,
the veins in my forearms
the inside and the out,
my darkening skin.

Spray of Mist

In the winter when it is cold
and dark early and you
are not here to speak to
your brown eyes remain
imprinted.

Light rain falls.
Not enough for anyone
to notice. Not enough
for anyone to care.

Cold filters out your breath,
mists the edges of air,
thin edges, white clouds
spraying out over the horizon.

Saugatuck

Fall's cool air across my chest
over my back and shoulders.
Three deer in the woods at the side of the road.
So much of life is loss.

Someone lives to be one hundred.
Someone lives to be thirty.
A young boy not yet fourteen
a baby girl, two. Childbirth. Rebirth.

Turtles bask on the banks of the Saugatuck.
White pines tower seventy feet above.
Blue Spruce thrive where no people live.
In a Connecticut river valley,
the face of a man
who has lost his child.

The Red Barn

Four hundred years ago no people lived
in these woods.
The turn of your body to the side
reveals a silhouette, softly curving
toward the branches.

Three hundred years ago Native Americans camped here.
Hunting deer at dusk. Lighting small fires.
Your great-great-great grandmother glad for the food.

Two hundred years ago white men settled.
She came down from the hills along a rocky path.
Long dark hair hanging over her shoulders.

The red barn stands surrounded by lodge pole pine.
One hundred feet from the barn, a house.
Ten cows in a small field.
In the living room an Amaryllis blooms.

Overland Trail

A snowstorm rages in my mind.
Outside clear blue sky,
freezing cold, winds gusting to forty.

What about you does this tell me?
Who exactly is the you?
Who exactly are you?

My friend said, *you should write children's books.*
That's what people want.
You could make so much money.

Looking out the window of our house
on Overland Trail in Colorado
there is nothing about children's books.

Only flat open plain, some rocks,
the foothills in the distance.
Up Poudre Canyon things change.

The deer antler in the wood,
Horsetooth Reservoir
dotted with small homes and cabins.

No heat on Overland Trail.
I see you naked, shivering
in the morning.

The wind gusts die down.
The snowstorm fades.
Clear blue sky drifts into darkness.

Sara in Winter

In winter in Telluride
before the skiers come, waitressing
at 6 a.m., only locals in the café.

So many things are so important. Hot
coffee, ketchup on the table, not
confusing decaf with regular.

Early morning light surrounds her.
The sun is so beautiful, sweet
sounds of clanging silverware. Sara says,

I wonder if any of it is worth it? I wonder
what the end result will be? I need
someone to understand me.

In summer in Ouray
when the hot springs are too hot, searching
at 7 a.m., only myself to turn to. She says,

Everyone has their own demons to face. Lies,
doubt, loneliness, dark eyes gazing
out from the hot springs, swallowing

my breath, my thoughts plunging
to the bottom of the springs, to the rocks
and crevices, where everything is lost.

Snow Hangs on the Branches of Evergreens

I fell in love with you
over and over again
until finally it was time
for breakfast. Since I mostly eat
oatmeal with blueberries, there were
no waffles or pancakes to share.

Though if you had said, *let's have waffles,*
I would have, just to be closer to you.
The distance between us will always be there,
breakfast, lunch, the base of the Eiffel Tower,
the canals of St. Petersburg.
Running at 7 a.m. on the cobblestones
alongside old Amsterdam canals,
I step to avoid the bicycling city.
We should have had the waffles and not
argued. We should have gone further south
before heading north.

Snow hangs on the branches of evergreens
and outlines the bottom of my window.
When I look into your eyes
I see New Hampshire, Connecticut, a small valley,
a wood shingled house set back from the heartache
of life. All those pins that prick your heart
disappear.

The Wind Took You Away

I had wanted to have lunch with you
for so long and then
you came to me, hungry
craving, reaching out a hand.

Was it the food or something more?
Maybe neither. Maybe it was a crossroad
in your life. A turning point you don't yet
know about. Maybe it was me, confused about
lunch or dinner. After all, 4 o'clock, what is that?

In the middle of a sea, a desert, a vast open plain,
a valley stretches out in front of us.
Acres of timber will not satisfy hunger.
The body needs protein, flesh and blood,
heart and muscle, spirit and soul.

The body needs warmth at night,
dry when it rains,
no wind when it's windy.
And then the wind took you away.

Brooklyn

This poem for Brooklyn
is about you   it is never
about I   it is never
they or them or it
or us
it is you
and always has been

Down these concrete steps
narrow streets alleys
wide avenues parkways
parks seem to go back
one hundred years
before there was cobblestone
dirt lanes crossed everywhere

God the eagle has soared
and landed in Brooklyn
this thing you call Brooklyn
moonscape landscape building scape
fire and fire escape

Brooklyn Eagle Walt Whitman
wonder of science   There is no art
to it To this landing
to this falling
down stoops
and broken pavement
steps and
broken concrete

How can you say this is Brooklyn
when it's not
How can you say endless
when it's that

Oak and elm and flowering cherry
glacial ravine, rock out cropping
overpass and under pass
squirrel and pizza,   squirrel
eating pizza I swear no one would believe
it   and you Blackbird   trying so hard
to get into my poem

Lido Beach

I know you want to kiss me
Five ships on the horizon

I know you want to kiss me
Gulls on the shore

I know you want to kiss me
My neck tightens

I know you want to kiss me
Never here before

I don't think you want to kiss me
Ocean deep and green

I don't think you want to kiss me
You know exactly what I mean

I don't think you want to kiss me
Wooden sailboat in the bay

I don't think you want to kiss me
Save it for another day

Syracuse

for my father

And like a field
so far from view
I saw a shadow and knew
it was you.

Gray clouds
and cold damp days
filled with smoke,
a mottled haze.

A stony hilly street
leaves me numb
and in a daze.

Walking streets so late at night
a steep hill, stairs of flight
walking streets in early morn
a dewy mist, a shapeless form.

Out in the field behind my house
a tractor stalls, a lonely mouse.
A hawk swoops down and in a blink
that mouse is gone, ground stained pink.

Running Water

High
in the mountains
a swallow

spirals
her wings
and curls away

above
a tumbling, sparkling
spring.

Nothing is static.

Low fields
thick with wheat
fall to the thresher

and crumble
beneath his tractor
tires.

The Poudre River runs
up canyon.

Geese call geese
and gather together
gray-backed,

and green-necked
and great
in wild number.

Iced water
runs fast
past

spiked reeds reel
up crystal clear,

white caps
crowning white air.

Gold
lingering
in the after-

noon light
glazes the Poudre
perfectly.

The water crackles.

Her lips ripe,
split logs wedged
across the water

we crossed.
Taking her hands
I taste the wild water

and swallow.
The dark lily opens
her heavens.

Gypsy Book of Life

after visiting San Diego

I leave the window open a crack,
some fresh air as you suffocate.
The last bits of air escape your lungs.
At the cemetery sometimes
I see a red fox.
The wind blows a warm breeze.
The years pass peacefully.

Sometimes it is a different world, a different life
a larger house, more to do.
Silent and still she sleeps by my side.
Some things are starting to make sense
the red fox, a small house cat, brown
bunnies on my lawn.

Glass kitchen doors to the patio are wide open
whispering so as not to wake a husband or daughter.
There are no bugs on the Frangipani.
There are not as many bugs as in New York.
The Swallows of Capistrano no longer return.
The Admirals of Coronado live like lords and kings.
San Diego Bay is awash in warships and sunlight.
Where did the homeless go?

She says, *would you like the newspaper or the comics?*
I say, *not the comics. You can leave the newspaper
on the kitchen table.* She says,

I thought you might like something light.
I say, *there is nothing light anymore.* She says,
I know but I want the kids to feel positive about the future.

Meditation

Everything else goes on
like nothing ever happened.

Down syndrome.
Stage three breast cancer.

A daughter who thinks she is a man.
A man who thinks he is a woman,
a controlling take over your mind
kind of person.

A back that won't stop hurting, pain
from every direction, day and night
a broken hip, crushed pelvis, sprained wrist
limp, hanging useless, wrapped in tape.

Losing a child puts you closer to God.
Not in a church or temple sort of way,
in your heart.

Why did he take him?
Why did she take her?

I speak for many when I say
oceans never end, seas
are not always calm.

Disconnect

As the north wind blows over
the tops of trees and across the field, time
passes, relationships change, phones disconnect.

One morning you get to work early and find
you no longer have a job. One evening
you come home to find intruders

have eaten your ripe tomatoes, the ones
you grew yourself in the garden
behind your house.

Someone else left a notice in your mailbox,
a poem perhaps about Spain or Italy. A poem
they wrote, or maybe Garcia Lorca, maybe

it was "Black Trouble" from the Gypsy Ballads
which ends "the far-off dawn." In the event
it is something more serious, unspeakable

tragedy, trampled down flowers, a child
whose heart is not well, blueberries
spilled across the kitchen floor, melted

chocolates, death by disease: Nothing
compares to the arc of light over
glacial lakes, clear light as if

the veins flowing to your heart opened, as if
I actually knew where I was going
and went there.

Setback

I just want to touch you lightly,
run the back of my hand over your cheek,
watch your ankles as you walk away.

Suddenly it's 3 a.m. and I can't fall back to sleep.
Loud voices fade, squirrels are talking.
It is hard to understand them.

Early spring cardinals are chirping.
It is hard to see where they are. In the shower
your hair hangs down over your shoulders,
your shoulders beading

under the force of steam.
Three different sets of friends
have experienced pain and grief and loss.
Step off the curb and turn an ankle,
slip in the market and rupture a disc,

open a can and slice your finger.
Suddenly the light at the top
of the Empire State Building is green.
The World Trade Center is no more.
A piece of my heart was torn away
like the limb from my white pine.

Thor's Hammer

It would have to be
the A-frame in Connecticut.
A large one, still
three bedrooms, an office library
scaled back acreage
because thirteen will never happen.

It would have to be
two girls and a boy running
in the woods, searching
for those snakes
I am afraid of.

It would have to be
deer and fox in winter
screech owl at night
red tail hawk in daylight.
More than one cat.
More than one dog.

I remember reading *Eleven* by Sandra Cisneros
about a girl's unhappy eleventh birthday.
She thinks back to when she was
five and six and seven and eight and nine and ten and how
all those years stay part of you.

It would have to be love. So
many people coming together
into one love and then
with no warning
it just drops on you
like Thor's hammer.

Peconic Bay

At night I relive my life in dreams.
All the people I know wake early or
late, get up go out, sit around.

All day a golden light, last day
together. The light comes from within.
I steal glances at the ocean, the bay

try to explain, try to touch you.
The ocean laps at the shore.

On our backs in tall fields
green trees form a canopy. Yellow
leaves float down between

hundreds of oak and elm.
A sliver of sun filters through.

Radiators

There are secrets in the garage.
Pieces of my life in the shed.

My son's ice skates and skis,
my daughter's memory box.

The river opens into a valley.
My home sits above the river
looks down the valley.

On a rainy morning
the canals of Amsterdam are muddy and gray.

My son's expensive racing bicycle
rests in the shed.

Outside, heavy rain
borders on wet snow. The deck is awash

in foam and sleet. Finally
the radiators are working.

Spring at the Cemetery

Water between the stones
trickles along the road.

This is the peaceful time.
If it rains, soil settles. In winter

ground freezes. It's the same
everywhere. Cracks open.

Cemetery men fill them in.
Everyone wants to be heard.

Even those that have passed.

Almost Done

I have never been to Central Park West
except that one time when
I was looking at the Dakota with you.

I have never been to Columbus Circle except
that one time when we sat on the steps of
the monument and tried to avoid
rough looking men.

I have never been to Washington Square Park
except that one time when we were in Greenwich Village and
had espresso at Café Reggio.

I have never been to the Brooklyn Promenade except
that one time we went to the River Café
with Stephanie and had a chocolate dessert
the shape of the Brooklyn Bridge.

I have never been to Columbia University
or Harlem or Spanish Harlem
except for the few years I studied writing there and
the one night we drove down from Syracuse for a concert.

I met a lot of poets at Columbia,
in the Village, at Syracuse and in Colorado.
Famous poets, published poets:

Ted Berrigan, Anne Waldman, Dee Snodgrass, Donald Justice,
Richard Howard, Mary Crow. Richard Howard liked me
when he heard I was a construction worker but
stopped liking me when I became a travel agent.

I have never been to Penn Station except
that one time on the express train moving slowly
through Jamaica,
trying to find enough air to breath, trying to find
a place to sleep uninterrupted by dreams.

Back to the Beginning

This morning
I saw the moon in your window.

The blur of movement becomes
a bare branched tree, winter gray
no leaves, the movement of waves.

Alone at last in a place like this, foggy
no clocks, your rock hard face, taut
sky camouflaging white concrete, smashed

against a shoreline. Time slows down.
Life has come full circle, back to the beginning.
No clocks.

Sometimes change comes hard, suddenly
and you know it. Sometimes
change happens without you realizing.

People want to be remembered. Create
art so as not to be forgotten.
Worship deities to understand,

commune with nature and music.
What is out beyond the sea is liquid
swallowed, surrounded, soundless, undulating.

I See Shadows

In Greece, mountains of rock,
loose shale and slides,
iron ore, caves, uncertainty.

Small patches of green.
Lonely shoots flutter in time.
Early morning reflects gray light.

Red Chianti from Florence.
Dry sweet wine from 1994, hand bottled
labels, a neat combination of script and print.

When I blew you a kiss, miles away
softest wind carried it to you.
I could feel you feeling it

on your cheek.
I can see you touching it.
I see shadows, sideways
from the corners of my eyes.

Cheyenne, Wyoming

Eagle Wing stretches
searching out Bison above
the plains. Crazy Horse dead.
Sitting Bull. Cochise. Satanta of the Kiowa.
Coyote bone whistle. Eagle feather.
Wind whistling through the round
hole in my stomach. Cheyenne
Wyoming. Sunrise. Clear channel a.m. radio.
Wind River creek. Rainy Mountain creek.
All those dead
Buffalo bones heaped in piles
alongside the roadway.
Crazy drunks floating above the
Prairie. Cottonwood bark.

About the Author

Stuart P. Radowitz, a Long Island poet, has had a long and successful career in business and education. He is presently an instructor in the English Department at Molloy College, teaching creative writing and critical reading classes.

Stuart looks to nature as a canvas for spirituality and a portal to our souls. His travels have influenced much of his writings. Stuart has been published in various literary journals and has read his poems throughout the New York area including his poem "Closer to God" at Bethany French Baptist Church in Jamaica, NY in honor of Dr. Martin Luther King Jr. and his poem "Peconic Bay" at the Walt Whitman Birthplace in Huntington, NY in honor of Walt Whitman's Bicentennial. He also participated in poetry readings for Poets in Nassau, Bards Initiative's annual book launch, Nassau County Poet Laureate Society's annual book launch, Mid-Island Y JCC's poetry reading series, Performance Poets Association, and the Molloy College poetry series.

Stuart has his master's degree in creative writing and literature from Colorado State University and has studied as an undergraduate at Syracuse University with W. D. Snodgrass, Philip Booth, and Donald Justice.

He lives with his wife Sherry, Violet the cat, two aquatic turtles (Mr. & Mrs. T), and his giant 60lb. tortoise, Snuffy. His daughter Stephanie, her husband Dave, granddaughter Emily, and grandson Ryan live in the Connecticut hills.

www.ingramcontent.com/pod-product-compliance
Lightning Source LLC
Chambersburg PA
CBHW032029090426
42741CB00006B/792